Festivals *of the* World

PERU

Gareth Stevens Publishing
MILWAUKEE

Written by
LESLIE JERMYN

Edited by
SUSAN MCKAY

Designed by
HASNAH MOHD ESA

Picture research by
SUSAN JANE MANUEL

First published in North America in 1998 by
Gareth Stevens Publishing
1555 North RiverCenter Drive, Suite 201
Milwaukee, Wisconsin 53212 USA

For a free color catalog describing Gareth
Stevens' list of high-quality books and multimedia
programs, call
1-800-542-2595 (USA)
or 1-800-461-9120 (Canada).
Gareth Stevens Publishing's Fax: (414) 225-0377.
See our catalog, too, on the World Wide Web:
http://gsinc.com

© TIMES EDITIONS PTE LTD 1998
Originated and designed by
Times Books International
an imprint of Times Editions Pte Ltd
Times Centre, 1 New Industrial Road
Singapore 536196
E-mail: te@corp.tpl.com.sg
Printed in Singapore

Library of Congress Cataloging-in-Publication Data:
Jermyn, Leslie.
Peru / by Leslie Jermyn.
p. cm.—(Festivals of the World)
Includes bibliographical references (p. 27) and
index.
Summary: Describes how the culture of Peru is
reflected in its many festivals, including the Festival
of the Sun, Corpus Christi, and Puno Day.
ISBN 0-8368-2006-1 (library binding)
1. Festivals—Peru—Juvenile literature.
2. Peru—Social life and customs—Juvenile
literature. [1. Festivals—Peru. 2. Holidays—Peru.
3. Peru—Social life and customs.]
I. Series.
GT4839.A2J47 1998
394. 26985—dc21   97-27949

1 2 3 4 5 6 7 8 9 01 00 99 98

CONTENTS

It's Festival Time . . .

The word in Spanish for "festival" is *fiesta* [fee-EST-a]. Most fiestas in Peru are part of a religious event. Once the church bells have rung to signal the end of a holiday service, the music starts up and the fireworks explode. Although there is a serious reason for all the festivals, Peruvians never miss an opportunity to celebrate. So, why don't you come along and celebrate, too! It's fiesta time in Peru.

WHERE'S PERU?

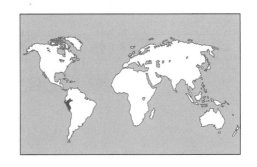

Peru is in South America, south of the equator. Peru shares borders with Ecuador and Colombia in the north, Brazil in the east, and Bolivia and Chile in the south. To the west is the Pacific Ocean. The capital city is Lima on the west coast.

There are three types of climate in Peru. Along the coast, it's very hot and dry like a desert. In the Andes Mountains, which run through the middle of Peru, it is much colder than the coast. In the northeast, the weather is hot and wet. This area is part of the Amazon Jungle.

Who are the Peruvians?

There are many different cultural groups in Peru. The two biggest groups are the *mestizos* [mess-TEE-zos]—a mixture of Spaniards and Indians—and the **Quechua** [KAY-choo-a] Indians. The Spaniards came to Peru in 1532, 40 years after Columbus discovered America. The Spanish leader was Francisco Pizarro. When Pizarro arrived, he found that most of the Quechua Indians lived high up in the mountains. He was surprised to discover that the Indians had roads, buildings, and a very organized society headed by a king. The king was called the Inca. Today, we call the whole society by the name *Incas*.

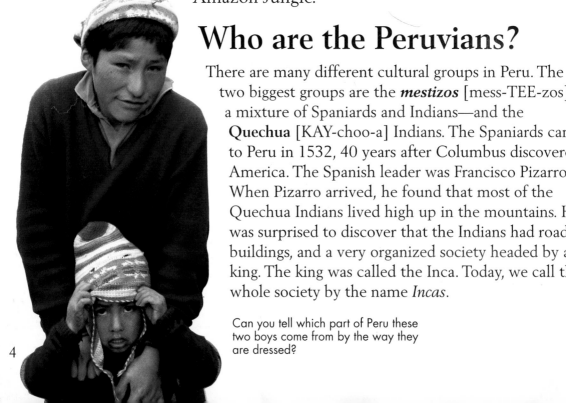

Can you tell which part of Peru these two boys come from by the way they are dressed?

4

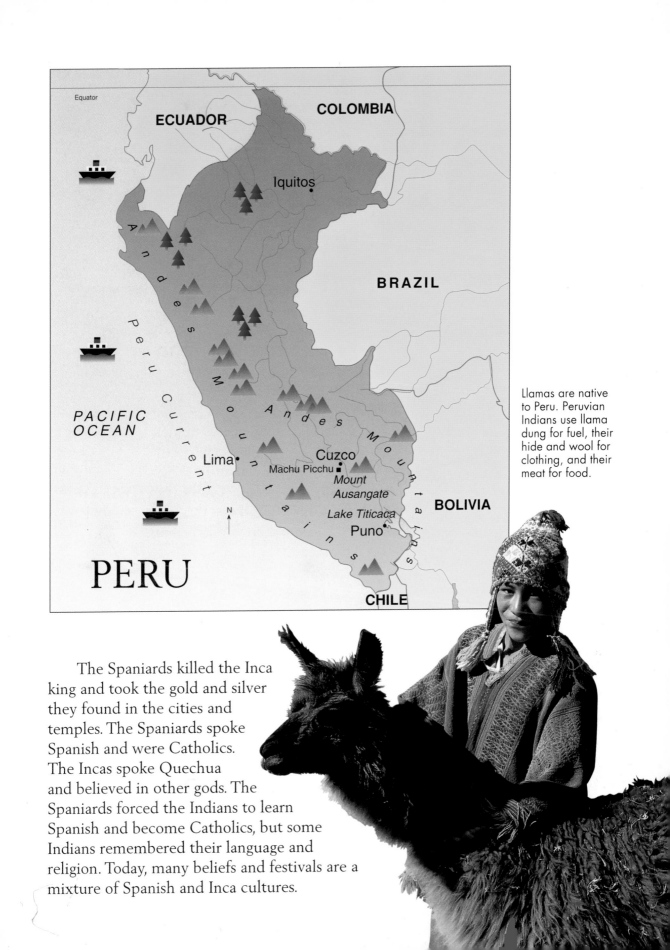

Equator

ECUADOR

COLOMBIA

Iquitos

BRAZIL

A
n
d
e
s
M
o
u
n
t
a
i
n
s

Peru Current

PACIFIC
OCEAN

Lima

Cuzco

Machu Picchu

Mount Ausangate

Lake Titicaca

Puno

BOLIVIA

N

PERU

CHILE

Llamas are native to Peru. Peruvian Indians use llama dung for fuel, their hide and wool for clothing, and their meat for food.

The Spaniards killed the Inca king and took the gold and silver they found in the cities and temples. The Spaniards spoke Spanish and were Catholics. The Incas spoke Quechua and believed in other gods. The Spaniards forced the Indians to learn Spanish and become Catholics, but some Indians remembered their language and religion. Today, many beliefs and festivals are a mixture of Spanish and Inca cultures.

WHEN'S THE FIESTA?

SPRING

- ✪ **DÍA DE LA VIRGEN DE MERCEDES (VIRGIN OF MERCY DAY)**—She is the special saint of the army. Her day is celebrated with military parades.
- ✪ **EL SEÑOR DE LOS MILAGROS (OUR LORD OF MIRACLES)**
- ✪ **TODOS SANTOS (ALL SAINTS' DAY)**
- ✪ **TODOS MUERTOS (ALL SOULS' DAY)**—This is the day when people bring food and drinks to the graves of friends and family members who have died.
- ✪ **PUNO DAY**
- ✪ **FIESTA DE LA PURÍSIMA CONCEPCIÓN (FESTIVAL OF THE IMMACULATE CONCEPTION)**—This is the celebration of the day when Mary became pregnant with Jesus.

Paint your face and join in the celebrations!

SUMMER

- ✪ **NAVIDAD (CHRISTMAS)**—On Christmas Eve, people in Lima go to Midnight Mass at Saint Peter's Church. On Christmas Day, there are bullfights and parties.
- ✪ **AÑO NUEVO (NEW YEAR'S DAY)**
- ✪ **DÍA DE LOS REYES (DAY OF THE KINGS, EPIPHANY)**
- ✪ **CARNIVAL**—Throughout the month of February, people all over Peru have parties every Sunday. During these parties, people can throw water at each other!

Learn the steps at the Star Snow Festival on page 16.

AUTUMN

- ⊛ **SEMANA SANTA (EASTER)**
- ⊛ **PERUVIAN PASO HORSE EXHIBIT**—A breed of Peruvian horse is the focus of this celebration. There are shows of the horses and their special abilities.
- ⊛ **QOYLLUR RIT'I (STAR SNOW FESTIVAL)**
- ⊛ **CORPUS CHRISTI**
- ⊛ **MAY DAY**—This is International Labor Day—a public holiday in Peru.

How would you like to wear a costume like this one?

WINTER

- ⊛ **INTI RAYMI (FESTIVAL OF THE SUN)**
- ⊛ **SAINT PETER'S DAY**—Saint Peter looks after fishermen. On this day there are parades and celebrations in the villages along the coast where the fishermen live.
- ⊛ **FIESTAS PATRIAS (INDEPENDENCE DAY)**—The day that celebrates Peru's independence from Spain. Everyone has a day off work, and there are military parades in the main cities.
- ⊛ **SANTA ROSA DE LIMA**—Saint Rosa is the saint who looks after the Americas. On this day, she is taken out of her church in Lima and paraded around the city. Everyone lines the streets to watch or follow the parade.

THE FESTIVAL OF THE SUN

At the end of June each year, Cuzco, the ancient capital city of the Incas, hosts the Festival of the Sun. The festival is called *Inti Raymi* [EEN-tee RYE-mee] by Peruvians. *Inti* means "sun" and *Raymi* means "dance" in Quechua—the language of the Incas. Inti Raymi is the Incan New Year's party. It's the most important festival for the Indians of Peru.

Offering food to the sun god.

The Inca emperor is carried into the fort on a sedan chair and guarded by real army troops dressed up in costumes.

The winter solstice

The earth goes around the sun once every 365 days, or once every year. Because the earth tilts a little, the northern hemisphere is closer to the sun for half the year. The southern hemisphere is closer for the other half. Peru is in the southern hemisphere, where winter runs from December to June. The winter solstice is the day when the sun is farthest from the earth. It is the longest night of the year. It is also the time when Peruvians celebrate the Festival of the Sun. Keep reading to find out why.

Inca beliefs

The Incas were mostly farmers who grew potatoes and corn. They harvested their crops in May just before the winter solstice. As the days became shorter through the summer, the Incas believed the sun god was getting tired and his strength was waning. They held a special ceremony in honor of the sun god. At the ceremony, they offered him something to eat to get his strength back. They offered their corn and potatoes to thank him for giving them crops to harvest. They also lit bonfires and let them burn through the night to help the sun god get started again. Some people burned their old clothes to celebrate the beginning of a new year.

About 50 years ago, the Quechua Indians started to celebrate Inti Raymi again, the same way their Incan ancestors did. The festival celebrated today is based on descriptions written down hundreds of years ago.

The dancers dress in hand-woven traditional clothes. The ceremony only lasts a few hours, but the celebrations will continue throughout the week in Cuzco.

The "Incas" pretend to sacrifice a llama or a goat to the sun god while the emperor looks on.

Fiesta time

The main festival ceremony takes place in the fort at Machu Picchu (Ancient Peak), where the remains of an ancient Inca city still stand. Quechua Indians dress up as Inca warriors and wear special masks for dancing. One man dresses as the Inca emperor and becomes king-for-a-day. He leads the people into the fort, where he makes the first offering to the sun god.

Everyone plays a role in this fantastic performance. Even the llamas are dressed up for the day. When the musicians start playing, it is a signal for the dancing to begin. The fort is filled with people selling crafts and food.

Once the ceremony is over, after about three hours, everyone heads back down the mountain to Cuzco's main square. But the festival isn't over yet! Over the course of the next week, a giant fair takes place in Cuzco, and the dancing and partying continue late into the night.

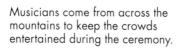

Musicians come from across the mountains to keep the crowds entertained during the ceremony.

Listen to a story…

The Incas believed they were descendants of the sun and moon gods. This is the story of their birth. One day, a long, long time ago, the sun and the moon decided to have children of their own. They made Manco Capac and his sister, Mama Ocllo Huaco, the first king and queen of the Incas.

Manco Capac was given a golden stick by his father, the sun. He was told to leave Lake Titicaca, where he was born, and find a new home. He had to push the stick into the ground everywhere he traveled. When the stick went in easily, he would know he had found a good place to live. He walked and walked and finally came to Cuzco. When he pushed his golden stick into the earth, it went in very easily. Later on, Cuzco became the capital city of the Incas and the center of all Incan civilization. You can find Cuzco on the map on page 5.

Think about this

Two special days tell us when the seasons change. These are called solstices. One is on December 21st, and the other is 6 months later on June 21st. In Peru, June 21st is the day with the fewest hours of sunlight. What day has the most hours of sunlight for us? What day has the fewest hours of sunlight for us? Does anyone you know celebrate these days?

Girls performing in Cuzco's main square during the festivities.

CORPUS CHRISTI

Corpus Christi is a Catholic festival celebrated on a Thursday, 60 days after Easter. Many Catholic countries around the world celebrate Corpus Christi, but in Peru, it's a very big festival. People who live in and around Cuzco hold the biggest and most famous Corpus Christi celebration of all!

The party starts early

The excitement begins the day before the big event at 4 o'clock in the morning. All the church bells in Cuzco ring to wake everyone up. The people have to get up early to clean all the streets and prepare food and drinks for the big day. In the main square of Cuzco, called the Plaza de Armas, special altars are made for all the statues of saints that will be brought in from other neighborhoods and villages.

Left: Young boys are chosen to help the priest with the church services. They wear special red robes for the occasion.

Opposite: Some of the litters weigh up to a ton! The carriers have to bow at each of the altars as they pass, bearing all the weight on their shoulders. It is an honor to be a litter-bearer.

12

Each group of villagers dresses in different clothes to set themselves apart from the rest.

People come from far and wide

In the villages and churches outside Cuzco, the saints are dressed in festival clothes and put on special platforms so they can be carried into the city. The men of the village take turns carrying the saints (they're very heavy!), and the women walk beside them with food. Bands of musicians and dancers in fancy costumes join the parades. Saint Jerome is brought from the village of San Jerónimo, 3 miles (5 kilometers) away. Saint Sebastian comes from the church of San Sebastián. Saint Christopher is brought from the village of San Cristóbal, and Saint Blaise comes from San Blas. Finally, Saint Barbara is brought all the way from the village of Poroy, 80 miles (128 km) away!

All the villages have their own bands, litter-bearers, and dance troupes. These dancers are ready for the performance in the Plaza de Armas. They have been preparing for this for a long time!

A week-long party

By Wednesday night, all the saints have arrived in the main church, the Church of Santa Clara. This is where the special saint of Cuzco, the Virgin of Bethlehem, is waiting for them. The saints are kept all together in the church for the night. People believe they will spend the night talking about what has happened since the last Corpus Christi.

The next day, Corpus Christi, all the saints are moved in a long parade from the church through the city to the Plaza de Armas. The plaza is full of people watching the parade. The saints will stay in Cuzco for a week. During this time, there are more parades, special religious ceremonies, and lots of eating, drinking, and dancing. The dancers practice all year for this festival. One of the favorite festival drinks in Peru is called **chicha** [CHEE- cha]. It's a type of beer made from corn.

After a week of parties, the saints are carried back to their villages. They will have to wait another year until they can meet again in Cuzco!

Dancing in the Plaza de Armas. Corpus Christi is one of the most colorful of Peru's many festivals.

Think about this

When Corpus Christi was first celebrated in Peru, it was a very small festival. Finally, the Spanish priests discovered that the Indians preferred Christian festivals if they were colorful and fun. So, the priests dressed the saints in beautiful clothes and held parades to get the Indians interested. Today, it is one of Peru's biggest festivals.

15

THE STAR SNOW FESTIVAL

In Quechua, the Star Snow Festival is called Qoyllur Rit'i. It's called *Star* (Qoyllur) because at this time of year a special group of stars called the **Pleiades** [PLEE-a-dees] rises in the night sky. It's called *Snow* (Rit'i) because the Indians believe the snow from a certain mountain is very special, and they collect it during the festival. The Star Snow Festival is celebrated about the same time of year as Corpus Christi, but it's a very different kind of festival.

Feathers and wool

The Star Snow Festival takes place about 50 miles (80 km) east of Cuzco in the Andes Mountains. Indians come from all over Peru to take part in this festival. They dress in special costumes. Some dress like jungle Indians with feathered costumes. They are called **chunchos** [CHOON-chos]. Some of the younger men dress in woolly costumes with ski masks. They are the **ukukus** [oo-KOO-koos], or bears, and they have a very special job during the celebration.

Indians dressed as chunchos gather for the Star Snow Festival. They perform special dances before and after the mountain climbing.

Lighting candles in the temple in honor of the mountain god.

The mountain god

The festival starts the night the Pleiades stars first become visible. Everyone walks through the night to reach a temple on a mountain called Ausangate. There they make offerings to the mountain god. These gifts include starfish and seashells brought all the way from the Pacific Ocean, cookies, dolls made of metal, candies, incense, llama fat, and leaves from a special plant called coca. They also build tiny houses and animal pens out of stones. This is the way they ask the mountain god to make their crops grow and their animals healthy.

Many people travel long distances to be at Ausangate for the festival.

The ukukus arrive at the top of the glacier by early morning. It is cold, and they are tired from walking all night, but they have a mission to complete.

Climbing the mountain

At about 2 o'clock in the morning, the bear-men, or ukukus, start to climb up the glacier on the mountain. A glacier is a big chunk of ice high up in the mountains that never melts. Every village sends some of their young men to be ukukus. They have to be very strong and healthy because the air is very thin at high altitudes. That means there isn't very much oxygen, which is what people need to breathe. It's also very cold at night on the ice.

At the top of the glacier, 16,000 feet (4,875 meters) above sea level, the ukukus put a big cross into the ice and offer more presents to the mountain god. Everyone prays for good weather and then climbs back down the glacier. On the way down, the ukukus cut some ice to bring back to their villages. They believe the ice is magical and can make sick people well again.

Ukukus carry the magic ice down from the mountain. To carry these blocks, the ukukus must be strong, young men.

The next morning

When the ukukus arrive back at the temple at the bottom of the mountain, they hold a special religious ceremony. They let the magic ice melt and boil the water. Then they mix in barley (a type of grain) to make a warm drink.

After drinking the potion, most people go home, but the dancers walk another 20 miles (32 km) to a village called Tayankani. Thousands of Indians dressed in colorful costumes come together there for a party. Some dance and sing, while others just enjoy the occasion.

Think about this
Peruvian Indians believe the mountains are gods called *Apus* [AH-poos], who can be either very nice or very naughty. When the Apus are nice, they provide lots of water for the corn and potato fields. When they are naughty, the Apus send hail storms, lightning, avalanches, or blizzards.

Dancing and singing, the Indians celebrate Qoyllur Rit'i.

PUNO DAY

O n page 11, we learned that the Incas believed their first king and queen were born on Lake Titicaca. Puno Day, on November 5, is their birthday party. It's called Puno Day because it happens in a place called Puno in southern Peru. Can you find it on the map on page 5?

The patterns on the couple's robes are typically Incan.

A party on the lake

The celebration starts on the island of Titicaca. Indians dress up as Manco Capac, the first Inca, and his wife, Mama Ocllo Huaco. They are

taken by boat to the shore of the lake at Puno. People wait for them on shore, playing music and dancing in colorful costumes. Indians come from all over southern Peru to celebrate this day!

Lake Titicaca is the big lake in the south of Peru. Peru shares the lake with Bolivia. Indians in Peru believe the lake is sacred because the sun god, moon goddess, and the first Inca king and queen were all born on islands in the lake. If you visited Lake Titicaca, you could go to the Island of the Sun and the Island of the Moon and see the temples built by the Incas.

The boat arrives at Puno.

Special boats

The boats used for this festival are called **balsas** [BALL-sahs], and they are made from a plant that grows along the shores of the lake. The plant, a kind of reed, is called **totora** [toe-TOR-ah]. The boats are made by tying the reeds together in large bundles. When they are dry, the bundles of reeds float and can carry people and even animals. Over time, the reeds get wet, and the boats sink. Then new boats are made.

The balsas are decorated with flowers and rugs before the king and queen are transported to Puno.

Special people

A special group of Indians live on the shores and islands of Lake Titicaca. They are called **Urus** [OOR-us]. They invented balsas to travel around the lake. They use totora reeds for other things, too. When the first Spaniards came to Peru, the Urus hid from them by building floating islands out of totora. Since the Spaniards didn't have boats, they couldn't catch the Urus on the lake!

Dancers of the devil in Puno

After the birthday ceremony, the Indians begin the celebrations. Puno is one of Peru's folk centers. Every year, hundreds of dances are performed, but the greatest are reserved for fiestas. One of the most popular dances is the Diablada [dee-ah-BLAH-dah], or the Dance of the Devil. Dancers wear masks and costumes that make them look as horrible as possible. Throughout the dance they twist their bodies in awful positions to try to scare the children—and they usually succeed!

The people of Puno are used to hard work. Fiestas are the time when everyone takes a break to enjoy the entertainment.

Think about this

The Puno Day celebrations are a very special kind of birthday party in honor of Manco Capac and Mama Ocllo Huaco. Do you celebrate any special birthdays in your country? Why are they important days? Who do they honor? How do you celebrate your own birthday?

Opposite: There is a different costume for each dance, but they are all colorful and elaborate. Just look at the detail!

Right: Costumes, such as this one, are very expensive. In fact, they may be the most valuable items a Peruvian family owns.

OUR LORD OF MIRACLES

If you were in Lima on October 18th and 19th, you would see a painting of Mary and Jesus being carried through the streets by men dressed in purple. All the houses would be decorated with purple cloth and purple flowers would fill the streets. For the whole month of October the painting is kept in the church of Las Nazarenas. Peruvians believe the painting protects them from the earthquakes that plague the region. Keep reading and find out why.

Here's what happened . . .

In 1655, there was an earthquake in Lima that destroyed the city. The only thing left standing was the wall of a church with a painting of Mary and Jesus on it.

In 1687, there was another earthquake, and many people were killed. The people of Lima paraded the painting through the streets and everyone kneeled down when it passed. The tremors stopped and no one else was killed! It was a miracle! Today, the painting is called Our Lord of Miracles.

Left: Musicians take part in the procession, too.

Opposite: Everyone wears purple during the celebration because all the priests in the church where the painting was found wore purple robes.

THINGS FOR YOU TO DO

The Incas had lots of stories about how the world was made. The story of the first Inca king and queen is related on page 11. Some of their stories explain how animals became special. For Peruvians, the most important animal is the condor. This is a huge bird that lives in the Andes Mountains. It's the national animal of Peru. Below you can read about the condor, mountain lion, fox, and parrot.

Tell an Inca story

A long time ago in Peru, the most powerful god was Viracocha. He liked to disguise himself so no one would recognize him. One day, he was disguised as a poor man when he saw a beautiful goddess sitting under a tree. Her name was Cauillaca. Viracocha changed himself into a beautiful bird and flew up into the tree. He picked a seed from the tree and it grew into a delicious fruit. He dropped the fruit into her lap. She couldn't resist the look and smell of the lovely fruit, so she ate it. This made her pregnant. A while later, when her son was born, she wanted to find out who the father was. She called all the gods together and asked who had given her the fruit. Viracocha, still disguised as a poor man, said it was him. But she didn't believe such a poor-looking man could be a god, so she ran away with her son to the ocean.

An Indian dressed as a condor for Carnival.

Viracocha tried to call her back, but she kept running. He changed himself back into a mighty god and started to follow. On the way, he asked the animals if they had seen her. The condor said if he hurried, he could catch her. Viracocha rewarded the condor by making it strong and punishing anyone who killed it. The fox told him he would never catch her. This made the god angry, so he gave the fox a bad smell. The mountain lion gave Viracocha good directions. It was rewarded with strength and beauty. Finally, the parrot told Viracocha that Cauillaca and her son had already gone into the ocean and the god of the ocean had turned them into islands. Viracocha was angry at hearing bad news, so he made the parrot's voice very loud and unpleasant. This way it could never hide in the jungle. Sadly, when Viracocha reached the sea, he saw that the parrot had told the truth. Even today, you can see the small islands off the coast of Peru that used to be Cauillaca and her son.

Now tell your own story

Use your imagination and think of a story about some of the animals you know. How did the skunk get its smell and its stripe? Why do bears sleep all winter? How can fish breathe under water? Why does the eagle have a white head? Why does the beaver have a flat tail? Can you think of any other special animals?

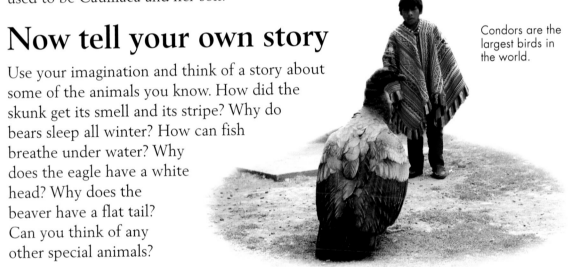

Condors are the largest birds in the world.

Things to look for in your library

Child of the Andes. National Film Board of Canada (video, 1985).

Eight Feet in the Andes. Dervla Murphy (John Murray, 1983).

Holidays, Festivals and Celebrations of the World Dictionary. Sue Ellen Thompson and Barbara W. Carlson (Omnigraphics Inc., 1994).

In the Shadow of the Incas. Gottfried Kirchner (video, 1989).

Lines to the Mountain Gods: Nazca and the Mysteries of Peru. Evan Hadingham (Random House, 1987).

Peru. Keiran Falconer (Times Books International, 1995).

Wonders of Man: Machu Picchu. John Hemming (Newsweek Book Division, 1981).

MAKE A SUN GOD MASK

The sun god was the father of the Incas. You can make your very own sun god mask by following the instructions on the next page.

You will need:
1. A paper or Styrofoam plate
2. Gold foil
3. Scissors
4. Yarn
5. String
6. Glue
7. A stapler
8. Shiny buttons or pieces of bright blue paper cut into small squares

4

6

3

7

8

5

1

2

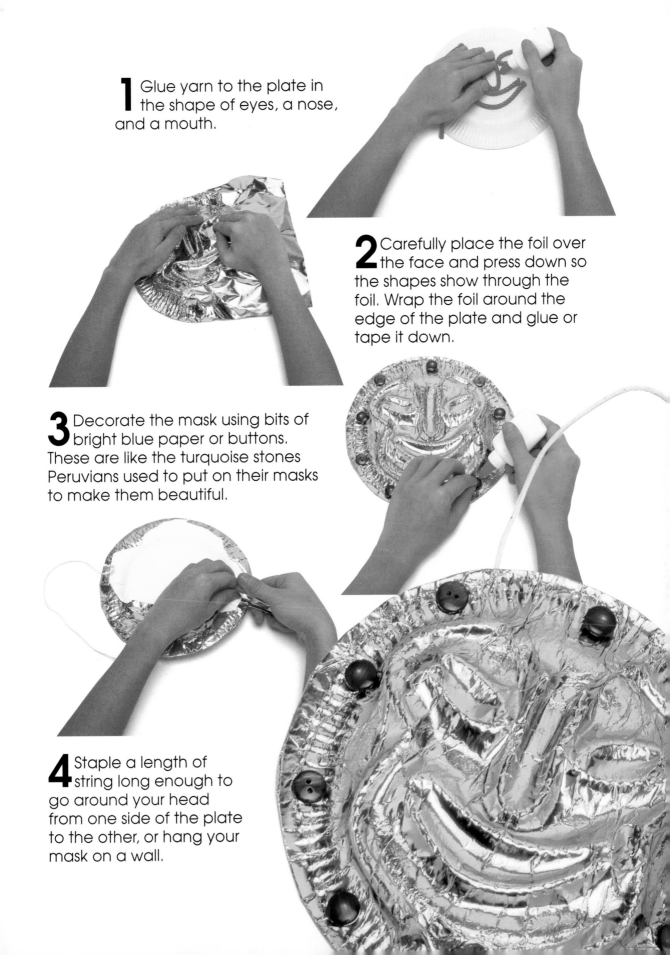

1 Glue yarn to the plate in the shape of eyes, a nose, and a mouth.

2 Carefully place the foil over the face and press down so the shapes show through the foil. Wrap the foil around the edge of the plate and glue or tape it down.

3 Decorate the mask using bits of bright blue paper or buttons. These are like the turquoise stones Peruvians used to put on their masks to make them beautiful.

4 Staple a length of string long enough to go around your head from one side of the plate to the other, or hang your mask on a wall.

MAKE NATILLA

Depending on where you live in Peru, there will be different kinds of food. If you lived in Lima, you would probably eat lots of fish from the ocean. If you lived high up in the mountains, you would eat lots of potatoes. One special treat that Peruvian children really enjoy is **natilla** [nah-TEE-ya], or caramel sauce. They like to put the sauce on bananas and peaches. Here's a recipe so you can try it yourself.

You will need:

1. 1 can (12 oz/360 ml) evaporated milk
2. 2 cups (480 ml) milk
3. ½ teaspoon baking soda
4. 1½ cups (350 grams) packed dark brown sugar
5. ¼ cup (60 ml) water
6. 3–4 cups (about 600 grams) of your favorite fruit
7. Measuring cups
8. Measuring spoons
9. A big pot
10. A medium-sized pot
11. A bowl
12. A wooden spoon
13. An oven mitt
14. A knife
15. A chopping board

1 Mix the evaporated milk, regular milk, and baking soda together in the big pot. Heat this mixture until it boils, then take it off the stove.

2 Mix the sugar and water in the medium-sized pot and heat over low heat. Stir until the sugar melts into the water.

3 Add the sugar to the milk mixture and cook everything to-gether over medium-low heat. Cook until sauce becomes thick and golden brown in color, about 1 hour. Put sauce in a serving bowl, cover, and refrigerate for 4 hours.

4 Cut fruit into pieces and cover with sauce. Then enjoy a Peruvian treat!

GLOSSARY

Apus, 19   Mountain gods who can bring either good or bad weather, depending on how they are treated.

balsas, 21   Boats made from reeds.

chicha, 15   A type of alcohol made from corn.

chunchos, 16   Indians dressed in feathered costumes.

mestizos, 4   Peruvians with Spanish and Indian blood.

natilla, 30   Caramel sauce eaten over fruit.

Pleiades, 16   A group of stars in the constellation Taurus.

Quechua, 4   The Indians of Peru and the language they speak.

totora, 21   Reeds that grow on the shores of Lake Titicaca used in making balsas.

ukukus, 16   Young men dressed in bear costumes with ski masks.

Urus, 21   A group of Indians who live on the shores and islands of Lake Titicaca.

INDEX